Let's go to

PERU

Keith Lye

Franklin Watts
London New York Sydney Toronto

Facts about Peru:

Area:
1,285,216 sq. km
(496, 225 sq. miles)

Population:
18,297,000

Capital:
Lima

Largest cities:
Lima (5, 259,000)
Callao (478,000)
Arequipa (447,000)
Trujillo (355,000)
Chiclayo (280,000)
Chimbote (216,000)

Official languages:
Spanish, Quechua

Religion:
Christianity

Main exports:
Minerals, especially copper, other metals, fish meal, coffee, cotton, sugar

Currency:
Inti

Franklin Watts
12a Golden Square
London W1

Franklin Watts Inc.
387 Park Avenue South
New York, N.Y. 10016

ISBN: UK Edition 0 86313 508 0
ISBN: US Edition 0 531 10363. 3
Library of Congress Catalog Card No: 86–51551

Typeset by Ace Filmsetting Ltd
Frome, Somerset
Printed in Hong Kong

Maps: Simon Roulstone
Design: Edward Kinsey
Stamps: Stanley Gibbons Limited
Photographs: Marion and Tony Morrison, South American Pictures 3, 4, 7, 8, 9, 10, 13, 14, 15, 16, 17, 19, 20, 21, 22, 23, 24, 25, 26, 27, 28, 29, 31; Keith Lye 5, 6, 12, 18, 30; Chris Fairclough 12

Front Cover: Marion and Tony Morrison
Back Cover: Marion and Tony Morrison

Peru is the third largest country in South America, after Brazil and Argentina. The high Andes Mountains run through western Peru. The highest peak, called Huascarán, is 6,768 m (22,264 ft) high. The Andes range separates the dry coastal plain from the hot rain forests in the east.

Some of Peru's mountains are volcanoes. When they erupt, they cause much damage. El Misti is a volcano which overlooks the city of Arequipa in southern Peru. It is 5,843 m (19,170 ft) above sea level.

Earthquakes are common. They also cause great damage. The picture shows earthquake damage to the Santa Catalina convent in Arequipa. This Spanish convent was built in the 16th century from a white volcanic rock.

Lake Titicaca is the world's highest large lake. It lies between two ranges of the Andes Mountains on Peru's border with Bolivia. The picture shows a floating island in Lake Titicaca, made from reeds by local Indians. They use reed canoes to fish.

Peru's coastal plain is a desert. At Nazca, in the south, long lines and huge drawings of such creatures as spiders have been marked on the ground. It has been suggested that aliens from space drew them, but most scholars think that Indians drew them long ago.

Peru lies in the tropics. The coast and the eastern plains have a warm climate, unlike the snow-capped Andes range. The eastern plains have plenty of rain. Thick forests, called selvas, cover large areas. The easiest way to travel there is by river.

The great Amazon River and many smaller ones drain into eastern Peru. Because travel is difficult, some Indians in the forests have never seen a foreigner. The Nahua Indians first came into contact with the outside world in 1986.

The picture shows some of the money used in Peru. The main unit of money is the inti, which is named after the Sun god of the ancient Incas. It replaced the sol in 1986.

WORLD
MAP
Peru

COLOMBIA
EQUADOR
Iquitos
Marañón R.
Amazon R.
Chiclayo
Andes Mountains
Trujillo
Huascarán
6,768m
Chimbote
BRAZIL
Ucayali R.
PERU
La Oroya
PACIFIC OCEAN
Callao
Lima
Machu Picchu
Cuzco
BOLIVIA
Nazca
Lake Titicaca
Arequipa

Lima, which stands on the coastal plain near the Pacific Ocean, is the capital of Peru. The picture shows the Palace of Justice in Lima. Peru is a republic. The President, the Head of State and the members of Parliament are elected to five-year terms.

Lima is by far the largest city in Peru. In recent years, people have flocked to Lima from the countryside. They hope to find work and enjoy a better life. But many have no jobs and live in slums. About two-thirds of Peruvians live in cities and towns.

Nearly half of the people of Peru are American Indians, and one out of every ten is of European descent. Around 43 out of every 100 people are of mixed Indian and European ancestry, like the mother and child shown here. They are called mestizos.

Europeans first went to Peru in the 1520s. In 1532–33, Spanish soldiers conquered Peru. They defeated the Indian Inca empire. The Incas had their capital at Cuzco. The picture shows the central square of Cuzco, where Inca palaces once stood.

The Incas ruled a great empire, which included parts of Colombia, Ecuador, Peru, Bolivia, Chile and Argentina. Ruins of Inca palaces, as here at Sacsayhuamán, near Cuzco, show their great skill as builders.

The Spanish soldiers destroyed many Inca towns and seized precious objects made of gold and other metals. But they never found Machu Picchu, an Inca town northwest of Cuzco. An American, Hiram Bingham, found it in 1911.

The Spaniards brought Christianity to Peru. About 95 out of every 100 Peruvians are now Roman Catholics. The picture shows a Roman Catholic church on the main square of Iquitos, a busy river port on the Amazon River in northeastern Peru.

This statue in Lima shows a Peruvian hero, José de San Martín. He was born in Argentina, and he opposed Spanish rule in South America. In 1820, he led an army into Peru and he declared Peru independent in 1821. The Spanish forces finally surrendered in 1826.

About two out of every five people in Peru work on farms. The chief food crops are bananas, beans, corn, potatoes and rice. Most farmers and farm workers are poor. Rich people, who belong to the upper and middle classes, live mainly in the cities.

Many farm workers live on large cooperative farms, where they work together and share the profits. The picture shows cotton being harvested on one of these large farms. Cotton, coffee and sugar are exported. Only 2 per cent of Peru is used to grow crops.

Grazing land covers 14 per cent of Peru. Many farmers keep cattle, goats and sheep. Others rear llamas, shown here, alpacas and vicuñas. Their wool is used to make textiles. Llamas are also used to carry goods.

Peruvians catch anchovies, tuna and other fishes in the Pacific Ocean. Fish meal is exported as a cattle feed. Overfishing and unusual weather conditions have reduced Peru's total catch in recent years.

Forests cover 55 per cent of Peru. Forestry is important in the Amazon region, where the wood is taken to sawmills by boat. Timber is used to make paper and furniture. The cutting down of trees has forced many Indians to give up their old ways of life.

Peru is rich in minerals. The picture shows a smelter at La Oroya, in the highlands east of Lima. Copper, iron ore, lead, oil, silver and zinc are all mined. Manufactures include refined metals, petroleum products, steel, textiles and processed food.

The law states that all children between 6 and 15 should go to school. Primary and secondary education is free at government schools, though many rich people pay fees to send their children to private schools. The best schools are in the cities.

The government has built many schools for poor Indian children in country areas in the last 20 years. But many places still do not have enough schools and teachers. As a result, about a fifth of Peruvians cannot read or write.

This mestizo family lives on the coast of Peru. Mestizos and people of European descent speak Spanish. The chief Indian languages are Quechua and Aymara. Various other Indian languages are spoken in the eastern forests.

Indian farmers sell their produce in the towns. The picture shows a Quechua Indian selling fruit. Peru produces a great variety of fruit and vegetables. Many people like their food seasoned with onions and hot red peppers.

Music and dance are popular pastimes in Peru. The musicians in this picture are using a mixture of traditional and western instruments. Many Peruvians listen to the radio. Television sets are less common. Many families cannot afford them.

Religious festivals are major events, when the rich and poor wear their best clothes. Tourists enjoy the festivals, together with Peru's beautiful scenery and historic sites. Tourist money is important, helping the government in trying to raise living standards.

Index